SCONES, MUFFINS & TEACAKES

*A collection of quick and easy teatime treats
too tempting to resist.*

M U R D O C H   B O O K S®

Sydney • London • Vancouver • New York

— MUFFINS —

Clockwise from top: Strawberry Muffins, Muffins, Apple and Spice Muffins

*M*uffins are generally classified as quick breads — quickly made and quickly eaten. They can be served for breakfast or lunch, with morning coffee or tea. Try them with soup or cheese and fruit for a light evening meal. Muffins can be sweet or savoury, high-fibre and healthy.

Muffins are surprisingly easy to make, even easier than scones. Simply follow the 'muffin method': add the combined liquid ingredients to combined dry ingredients with a few quick strokes. Use a fork for best results. The mixture should in fact still be lumpy and the result will be light, fine-textured muffins. Overmixing causes muffins to rise into a peak, producing long tunnels and a tough texture. If you're using fruit, cheese or bacon in a basic muffin mixture stir them into flour to avoid overmixing.

For baking use deep American-style muffin tins. Buy the deepest straight-sided tins with a non-stick finish. Drop the muffin mixture from a metal spoon evenly into the oiled tins. Brush oil into bottoms only, as unoiled sides allow batter to climb and form rounded tops while baking. Remember not to stir the muffin mixture again as you fill the tins. After baking, leave the muffins to cool in their tins for 3–4 minutes, and then carefully remove them to finish cooling on a wire rack.

Muffins are best eaten on the day they are made, served warm with butter. They can be stored in an airtight container for up to two days. Muffins freeze well for up to three months. Frozen muffins can be wrapped in foil and heated in a moderate oven for 10–12 minutes.

3 Stir gently with a fork until all dry ingredients are just moistened. Batter should look quite lumpy.

4 Spoon batter evenly into each muffin tin, filling two-thirds full. Bake 20–25 minutes until golden brown. Loosen muffins with a spatula and remove at once to a wire rack. Serve warm.

Strawberry Muffins

Preparation time: 20 minutes
Cooking time: 20 minutes
Makes about 12

3 cups plain flour
½ cup sugar
1 tablespoon baking powder
½ cup brown sugar
125 g butter, melted
3 eggs
1 cup milk
1½ cups strawberries, chopped
icing sugar to sprinkle

1 Preheat oven to 200°C. Brush oil into bottoms only of twelve muffin tins. Sift flour, sugar and baking powder into a bowl. Stir in brown sugar.

Muffins

Preparation time: 15 minutes
Cooking time: 25 minutes
Makes 12

1¾ cups self-raising flour
2 tablespoons caster sugar
1 teaspoon baking powder

1 egg, lightly beaten
¾ cup milk
80 g butter, melted

1 Preheat oven to 200°C. Brush oil into bottoms only of twelve 6 cm muffin tins.

2 Sift flour, sugar and baking powder in a bowl. In a small bowl combine egg, milk and melted butter. Mix well and add liquids all at once to flour mixture.

2 Combine melted butter, eggs and milk; stir into dry ingredients until just blended.
3 Fold in berries very lightly and carefully. Spoon into greased muffin tins until two-thirds full.
4 Bake for 20 minutes until browned. Sprinkle with icing sugar while hot. Serve hot with butter.

Apple and Spice Muffins

Preparation time: 20 minutes
Cooking time: 20 minutes
Makes 12

2 cups plain flour
1½ teaspoons baking powder
1½ teaspoons bicarbonate of soda
1 teaspoon cinnamon
¼ teaspoon nutmeg
⅓ cup brown sugar
1 cup chopped, peeled and cored apples
1 egg, lightly beaten
1 cup milk
2 tablespoons melted butter

1 Preheat oven to 200°C. Brush oil into bottoms only of twelve muffin tins.
2 Sift flour, baking powder, bicarbonate of soda, cinnamon and

nutmeg into a large bowl. Stir in brown sugar and apple.
3 Combine egg, milk and butter and mix well. Add egg mixture all at once to flour mixture. Stir gently with a fork until all ingredients are just moistened.
4 Spoon batter evenly into each muffin tin, filling two-thirds full. Bake 15–20 minutes until golden. Serve warm with butter.

Spiced Wholemeal Muffins

Preparation time: 20 minutes
Cooking time: 20 minutes
Makes 12

1 cup self-raising flour
¾ cup wholemeal self-raising flour
1 teaspoon mixed spice
½ teaspoon baking powder
½ teaspoon bicarbonate of soda
⅓ cup packed brown sugar
½ cup sultanas
1 egg, lightly beaten
1 cup buttermilk
80 g butter, melted

1 Preheat oven to 200°C. Brush oil into bottoms only of twelve

muffin tins.
2 Sift flours, mixed spice, baking powder and bicarbonate of soda into a large bowl. Stir in sugar and sultanas. Combine egg, buttermilk and melted butter and mix well.
3 Add egg mixture all at once to flour. Stir gently with a fork until all ingredients are just moistened.
4 Spoon batter evenly into each muffin tin, filling two-thirds full. Bake 15–20 minutes until golden. Serve warm with butter.

Blueberry Muffins

Preparation time: 15 minutes
Cooking time: 25 minutes
Makes 12

1¾ cups self-raising flour
2 tablespoons caster sugar
1 teaspoon baking powder
1 cup blueberries
1 egg, lightly beaten
¾ cup milk
⅓ cup butter, melted

1 Preheat oven to 200°C. Brush oil into bottoms only of twelve 6 cm muffin tins.

2 Sift flour, sugar and baking powder into a bowl and stir in blueberries. In a small bowl, combine egg, milk and melted butter and mix well. Add liquids all at once to flour mixture.
3 Stir gently with a fork until all dry ingredients are just moistened.

Batter should look quite lumpy.
4 Spoon batter evenly into each muffin cup, filling two-thirds full. Bake 20–25 minutes until golden brown. Loosen muffins with a spatula and remove at once to a wire rack. Serve warm with butter.

HINT

All ovens vary and not all thermostats are accurate. So always be ready to make slight adjustments to recommended cooking times and temperatures.

In the jar: Spiced Wholemeal Muffins; on the plate: Blueberry Muffins.

Cheese and Ham Muffins

Preparation time: 15 minutes
Cooking time: 25 minutes
Makes 12

1¾ cups self-raising flour
2 tablespoons caster sugar
1 teaspoon baking powder
1 cup grated Cheddar cheese
½ cup chopped ham
1 egg, lightly beaten
¾ cup milk
⅓ cup butter, melted

1 Preheat oven to 200°C. Brush oil into bottoms only of twelve 6 cm muffin tins.
2 Sift flour, sugar and baking powder in a bowl and stir in cheese and ham. In a small bowl combine egg, milk and melted butter and mix well. Add liquids all at once to flour mixture.
3 Stir gently with a fork until all dry ingredients are just moistened. Batter should look quite lumpy.
4 Spoon batter into each muffin tin, filling two-thirds full. Bake 20–25 minutes until golden brown. Loosen muffins with a spatula and remove at once to a wire rack. Serve warm.

Cornmeal Muffins

Preparation time: 15 minutes
Cooking time: 10 minutes
Makes 18 muffins

1½ cups flour
1 cup yellow cornmeal
½ teaspoon salt
4 teaspoons baking powder
¼ cup sugar
2 eggs
¼ cup oil
1 cup creamed corn
¾ cup milk
1 tablespoon chopped parsley

1 Preheat oven to 200°C. Grease well two deep patty trays. Sift flour, cornmeal, salt, baking powder and sugar into a large mixing bowl. In a large jug lightly beat eggs, oil, creamed corn, milk and parsley together to combine.
2 Make a well in the centre of the dry ingredients and pour in the liquid ingredients. Mix quickly with a fork to combine all ingredients. Do not overmix.
3 Spoon into patty tins and bake immediately for about 10 minutes. Serve warm.

Wholemeal Cheese Muffins

Preparation time: 20 minutes
Cooking time: 20 minutes
Makes 12

1 cup white self-raising flour
1 cup wholemeal self-raising flour
1 cup shredded Cheddar cheese
1 egg
60 g butter, melted
¾ cup milk
2 teaspoons French mustard
extra shredded cheese

1 Preheat oven to 200°C. Brush oil into bottoms only of twelve muffin tins.
2 Sift flours together in a large bowl and stir in cheese. Combine egg, butter, milk and mustard and mix well.
3 Add egg mixture all at once to flour mixture. Stir gently with a fork until all ingredients are just moistened.
4 Spoon batter evenly into each muffin tin, filling two-thirds full. Sprinkle each muffin with extra cheese. Bake 15–20 minutes until golden. Serve warm.

Back to front: Cheese and Ham Muffins, Cornmeal Muffins and Wholemeal Cheese Muffins

Carrot and Pineapple Bran Muffins

Preparation time: 30 minutes + 1 hour standing
Cooking time: 20 minutes
Makes 12

1 cup boiling water
1 cup natural bran
1 egg, beaten
⅓ cup brown sugar
½ cup shredded carrot
½ cup well-drained canned unsweetened crushed pineapple
2 tablespoons vegetable oil
1 cup plain flour
⅓ cup milk powder
1½ teaspoons baking powder
1½ teaspoons bicarbonate of soda
½ teaspoon ground ginger

1 Pour boiling water over bran; stand for 1 hour.
2 Preheat oven to 200°C. Brush oil into bottoms only of twelve muffin tins.
3 Stir egg, brown sugar, carrot, pineapple and oil into bran mixture. Mix well.
4 Sift flour, milk powder, baking powder, bicarbonate of soda and ginger into a large bowl. Add bran mixture all at once to flour mixture. Stir gently with a fork until all ingredients are just moistened.
5 Spoon batter evenly into each muffin tin, filling two-thirds full. Bake 15–20 minutes until golden. Serve warm with butter.

Carrot and Pineapple Bran Muffins

Banana Bran Muffins

Banana Bran Muffins

Preparation time: 20 minutes + 1 hour standing
Cooking time: 20 minutes
Makes 12

1 cup boiling water
1 cup natural bran
½ cup mashed ripe banana
1 egg, beaten
2 tablespoons vegetable oil
⅓ cup firmly packed brown sugar
1 teaspoon imitation vanilla essence
1 cup plain flour
⅓ cup skim milk powder
1½ teaspoons baking powder
1½ teaspoons bicarbonate of soda

1 Pour boiling water over bran in medium bowl. Stir and let stand for 1 hour.
2 Preheat oven to 200°C. Brush oil into bottoms only of twelve muffin tins. Add banana, egg, oil, brown sugar and vanilla essence to bran mixture and mix well.
3 Sift flour, milk powder, baking powder and bicarbonate of soda in a medium bowl. Add bran and banana mixture all at once to flour mixture. Stir gently with a fork until all ingredients are just moistened.
4 Spoon batter evenly into each muffin tin, filling two-thirds full. Bake 15–20 minutes until golden. Serve warm with butter.

— SCONES —

Scones with jam and cream

The ability to bake a good batch of high, light and golden scones has for generations been considered the test of a good cook. Here we show you how to bake perfect scones, time after time. There's no secret to perfect scones but there are a few points to remember.

As with any baking use the freshest ingredients. Self-raising flour is perfectly satisfactory for scones, though some believe plain flour and baking powder give a better result. Always add a little sugar to take away any floury taste from your scones. For lighter scones use half milk and half water. Sour cream, buttermilk and natural yoghurt can also be used, but water should be added to bring it to a watery consistency. Butter adds flavour and colour to scones and adds a little to their keeping quality.

Handle the scone dough lightly and work as quickly as possible to mix to a soft dough. Use only a small amount of flour on the kneading board and knead lightly until just smooth. For small batches of scones, press out dough with your hands to about 2 cm thick. Use a rolling pin for large quantities. Cut the scone dough with sharp metal cutters.

Before baking, brush scones with milk or buttermilk for golden shiny tops. Melted butter helps brown the tops but gives less shine. It is most important to cook the scones at a high temperature; a very hot oven of 220°C is best. After baking, scones may be cooled on a cake rack if you like them crisp, or wrapped in a clean tea-towel if you prefer softer scones.

Scones

Preparation time: 25 minutes
Cooking time: 12 minutes
Makes 12

2 cups self-raising flour
pinch salt, optional (see Note)
30 g butter, cut into small pieces
½ cup milk
½ cup water

1 Preheat oven to very hot (220°C). Sift flour and salt (if used) together into a large bowl. Add butter and rub in lightly using fingertips.
2 Combine milk and water. Make a well in the centre of the flour. Pour in liquid all at once, reserving about a teaspoon for glazing. Mix quickly to a soft dough.

3 Turn onto a floured board (use self-raising flour). Knead lightly. Press or roll out to form a round about 2 cm thick.
4 Cut using a floured plain round cutter or cut into triangles using a floured knife. Place on a greased oven tray and glaze with milk. Bake for 10–12 minutes or until scones sound hollow when tapped. Cool on wire rack. Serve with jam and cream.
Note. Salt is optional. However, it does enhance the flavour of the scones.

> ### HINT
> Handle the mixture with great care and a very light hand. If you are heavy-handed and mix or knead the dough too much, your scones will turn out very tough. Remember, undermixed is probably enough!

> ### HINT
> Don't add too much extra flour when kneading as a tougher, drier mixture will result.

1 *Add butter to flour and rub lightly, using fingertips, until mixture resembles fine breadcrumbs.*

2 *Pour combined milk and water into centre of the flour. Use a knife to mix to a soft dough.*

3 *Turn onto a lightly floured board and knead lightly. Press dough out to a thickness of 2cm.*

4 *Use a sharp cutter to cut dough into rounds.*

Apple and Cinnamon Scones

Apple and Cinnamon Scones

Preparation time: 35 minutes
Cooking time: 12 minutes
Makes 12

2 cups self-raising flour, sifted
30 g butter, cut into small pieces
⅓ cup caster sugar
1 green apple, peeled and grated
1 teaspoon ground cinnamon
1 egg, beaten
⅓ cup milk
1 tablespoon caster sugar, extra
¼ teaspoon ground cinnamon, extra

1 Preheat oven to very hot (220°C). Place flour in a bowl. Add butter and rub in using fingertips.

2 Stir in sugar, apple and cinnamon. Combine egg and milk. Make a well in centre of mixture. Pour in liquid all at once, reserving 1 teaspoon.

3 Mix to a soft dough. Turn onto a floured surface. Knead lightly. Press or roll out to form a round about 2 cm thick.

4 Cut into rounds using a floured plain cutter. Place on a greased baking tray. Glaze with remaining liquid. Sprinkle with combined extra sugar and cinnamon.

5 Bake for 10–12 minutes. Cool on a wire rack. Serve buttered.

13

Festive Scone Roll

Preparation time: 35
  minutes
Cooking time: 20
  minutes
Serves 10

2 cups self-raising flour
30 g butter, cut into
  small pieces
⅓ cup caster sugar
1 egg, lightly beaten
150 mL milk

Filling
90 g butter
1 tablespoon brandy
½ cup chopped red
  glacé cherries
½ cup chopped green
  glacé cherries
¼ cup chopped walnuts
icing sugar

1 Preheat oven to very
hot (220°C). Sift flour
into a large bowl. Add
butter and rub in lightly
with fingertips. Mix in
sugar.
2 Combine egg and
milk. Make a well in the
centre of the flour and
pour in liquid all at
once. Mix quickly to a
soft dough.
3 Turn onto a floured
board (use self-raising
flour). Knead lightly
and roll out to form
a rectangle about
1.5 cm thick.
4 To make filling, beat
butter and brandy
together until fluffy.
Spread over dough and
top with cherries and
walnuts.
5 Fold in short edges a
little to secure filling.
Roll up like a Swiss roll.
Place seam side down
on a greased oven slide.
6 Cut small slits in the
centre of the roll at
2 cm intervals and bake
for 20 minutes. Serve
warm dusted with icing
sugar.

HINT
Use sharp kitchen
scissors to cut slits
along the Scone Roll.

HINT
Scone dough can be
prepared in the food
processor. However,
scones made this way
are usually tougher
because of machine-
overmixing. If you
want to use the food
processor, use the
pulse action and
process only until
just mixed.

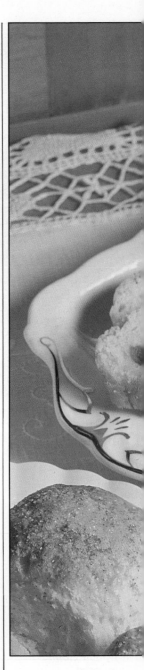

Festive Scone Roll

Cheese and Sesame Scones

Preparation time: 35
    minutes
Cooking time: 12
    minutes
Makes 12

2 cups self-raising flour
½ teaspoon salt
30 g butter, cut into
    small pieces
¾ cup milk

Topping
30 g butter
½ cup shredded
    Cheddar cheese
2 teaspoons mustard

2 teaspoons sesame
    seeds

1 Preheat oven to very
hot (220°C). Sift flour
and salt together into a
large bowl. Add butter
and rub in lightly using
fingertips.
2 Make a well in the
centre of the flour. Pour

Cheese and Sesame Scones

in liquid all at once and mix quickly to a soft dough.

3 Turn onto a floured board (use self-raising flour). Knead lightly. Press or roll out to form a round about 2 cm thick.

4 Cut using a floured plain round cutter. Place on a greased oven tray.

5 To prepare topping, melt butter gently over a low heat. Add cheese, mustard and sesame seeds. Allow cheese to melt. Mix together.

6 Spoon a little topping on each scone (make sure you use all the liquid). Bake for 10–12 minutes or until golden. Serve warm with butter.

Variation. Divide the dough into 12 portions and roll each portion into a long sausage shape. Twist each of the dough shapes into a 'knot' and bake as directed.

17

Clockwise from back left: Cheese and Chive Damper, Wholemeal Scone Round and Citrus Scone Round

Cheese and Chive Damper

Preparation time: 25 minutes
Cooking time: 20 minutes
Makes 1 Damper

2 cups self-raising flour
30 g butter, cut into pieces
1 cup grated Cheddar cheese
2 tablespoons grated Parmesan cheese
2 tablespoons chopped chives
½ cup milk
½ cup water
1 tablespoon grated Parmesan cheese, extra

1 Preheat oven to very hot (220°C). Sift flour into a large bowl. Add butter and rub in lightly with fingertips. Add cheeses and chives and mix well.
2 Combine milk and water. Make a well in the centre of the flour and pour in liquid all at once, reserving a little for glazing. Mix quickly to a soft dough.
3 Turn onto a lightly floured board. Knead lightly, press into a 20 cm round and place on a greased baking tray. Glaze with milk and sprinkle with extra cheese.
4 Bake for 15–20 minutes and serve sliced with butter.

Note. If desired, shape mixture into 6 rounds. Bake for 10–15 minutes.

HINT

We used half water and half milk in our scone dough as the water helps make a lighter product. All milk is better for sweet scones as it gives a richer result. You can use all water, half water and half milk or reconstituted milk. Another way is to add a tablespoon of powdered milk to the dry ingredients and then use all water as the liquid. All methods are suitable.

Citrus Scone Round

Preparation time: 20 minutes
Cooking time: 20 minutes
Makes 8 wedges

2 cups self-raising flour
60 g butter
⅓ cup wheatgerm
2 tablespoons chopped mixed peel
1 tablespoon caster sugar
2 teaspoons grated lemon rind
1 egg, beaten lightly
1 tablespoon lemon juice
3 tablespoons milk

1 Preheat oven to very hot (220°C). Sift flour into a large bowl, add butter and rub in lightly with fingertips.
2 Mix in wheatgerm, mixed peel, sugar and lemon rind. Combine egg, lemon juice and milk. Make a well in the centre of the flour and pour in liquid all at once. Mix quickly into a soft dough.
3 Turn onto floured surface (use self-raising flour) and knead lightly. Shape dough into a 20 cm round and place on a greased tray.
4 With a floured knife, cut completely through to bottom to make eight wedges. Glaze with a little milk.
5 Bake for 20 minutes. Cool on a wire rack for 5 minutes and serve with butter and marmalade.

HINT
Try this for a change: top casseroles or stewed fruit with sweet or savoury scone dough. Cook for 20–30 minutes.

Wholemeal Scone Round

Preparation time: 20 minutes
Cooking time: 20 minutes
Makes 8 wedges

2 cups wholemeal self-raising flour
1 cup self-raising flour
1 teaspoon cinnamon
¼ teaspoon nutmeg
¾ cup milk
2 tablespoons honey
45 g butter, melted
milk for glazing

1 Preheat oven to very hot (220°C).
2 Sift flours and spices into a bowl. Add rough fibre of wholemeal flour to bowl. Combine milk, honey and melted butter. Stir into dry ingredients and mix to a soft dough with a dinner knife.

3 Turn out onto a lightly floured surface and knead gently. Shape dough into a 20 cm round and place on greased tray.
4 With a floured knife, cut completely through to bottom to make eight wedges. Separate wedges slightly. Brush top with a little milk to glaze. Bake for 20 minutes or until pale gold.
5 Remove from oven and wrap in a clean tea-towel for 10 minutes before serving warm with lashings of butter.

HINTS
☐ Traditionally a scone is triangular in shape, made by shaping dough into a round and cutting into triangular sections from the centre.

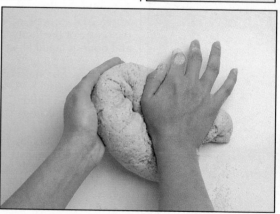

Step 1 Turn dough onto a lightly floured surface; knead gently.

Pumpkin Scone Wedge

Pumpkin Scone Wedge

Preparation time: 30 minutes
Cooking time: 25 minutes
Serves 6

30 g butter
2 tablespoons sugar
1 cup mashed, well-drained, cooked pumpkin
1 egg
2 cups self-raising flour
pinch salt
1/3 cup sultanas
milk for glazing

1 Preheat oven to hot (200°C). Beat together butter and sugar until creamy. Mix in pumpkin and egg.
2 Sift flour and salt and mix in together with sultanas.
3 Knead lightly on a floured surface. Pat into a 20 cm round and place on a lightly greased oven tray. Cut into eight sections almost to the bottom so that they can be pulled apart when baked. Brush with milk and bake for 20–25 minutes until cooked.

HINT
All scone recipes can be successfully doubled but the cooking time will be slightly longer.

Step 2 Shape dough into a 20 cm round. Cut completely through to make eight wedges.

21

Damper

Preparation time: 25 minutes
Cooking time: 20 minutes
Makes 1 Damper

2 cups self-raising flour
30 g butter, cut into
  small pieces
½ cup milk
½ cup water
sesame seeds

1 Preheat oven to very hot (220°C). Sift flour into a large bowl, add butter and rub in lightly with fingertips.
2 Combine milk and water, make a well in the centre of the flour and pour in liquid all at once. Mix quickly to a soft dough.
3 Turn onto a floured board (use self-raising flour). Knead lightly and form into a 20 cm round.
4 Place on a greased oven tray. Glaze with a little milk and sprinkle with sesame seeds.
5 Bake for 15 minutes. Reduce heat to moderately hot (190°C). Bake a further 5–10 minutes or until Damper sounds hollow when tapped. Serve the Damper warm and buttered as an unusual meal accompaniment.

Danish Scone Roll

Preparation time: 40 minutes
Cooking time: 20 minutes
Makes 12

2 cups self-raising flour
30 g butter, cut into
  small pieces
⅓ cup caster sugar
1 egg, lightly beaten
150 mL milk
Filling
125 g cream cheese, at

Clockwise from top left: Damper, Danish Scone Roll, Scones with jam and cream. Centre: Jam Pinwheel

room temperature
¼ *cup brown sugar*
½ *cup canned pie apple*
¼ *teaspoon cinnamon*
¼ *cup sultanas*

1 Preheat oven to very hot (220°C). Sift flour

into a large bowl. Add butter and rub in lightly with fingertips. Mix in sugar.
2 Combine egg and milk. Make a well in the centre of the flour and pour in liquid all at

once. Mix quickly to a soft dough.
3 Turn onto a floured board (use self-raising flour). Knead lightly. Roll out to form a rectangle about 1.5 cm thick.
4 Cream cheese and sugar together until fluffy. Spread over dough and top with apple. Sprinkle with cinnamon and sultanas.
5 Fold in short edges a little to secure filling. Roll up like a Swiss roll. Place seam side down on a greased oven slide.
6 Cut small slits in the centre of the roll at 2 cm intervals. Bake for 20 minutes. Serve warm with cream.

Pumpkin Scones

Preparation time: 35
  minutes
Cooking time: 12
  minutes
Makes 12

30 g butter
2 tablespoons caster
  sugar
½ cup mashed pumpkin
1 egg, lightly beaten
½ cup milk
2½ cups self-raising
  flour, sifted

1 Preheat oven to very hot (220°C). Cream butter and sugar

Pumpkin Scones, Sultana Scones,

23

together until light and fluffy. Mix in pumpkin, egg and milk.

2 Lightly fold in flour and mix until a soft dough is formed.

3 Turn onto a floured board (use self-raising flour). Knead lightly. Press or roll out to form a round about 2 cm thick.

4 Cut into rounds using a floured plain cutter. Place on greased oven tray. Glaze with a little milk. Bake for 10–12 minutes. Serve warm with butter.

HINTS
☐ Use the recipe for Pumpkin Scones but replace the pumpkin with ¼ cup mashed potato and ¼ cup mashed pumpkin to make Potato and Pumpkin Scones.

☐ Plan ahead by cooking a little extra of each vegetable for dinner the night before. Mash and refrigerate, covered, until required.

HINT
For a fruity pinwheel, use the same recipe but replace the jam with your choice of: ½ cup fruit mince; or 100 g glacé cherries, chopped, and mixed with ¼ cup chopped mixed nuts.

Jam Pinwheel

Preparation time: 30 minutes
Cooking time: 20 minutes
Makes 12

2 cups self-raising flour
30 g butter, cut into small pieces
⅓ cup caster sugar
1 egg, lightly beaten
150 mL milk
½ cup strawberry or other jam

1 Preheat oven to very hot (220°C). Sift flour into a large bowl. Add butter and rub in lightly with fingertips. Mix in sugar.

2 Combine egg and milk. Make a well in the centre of the flour and pour in liquid all at once. Mix quickly to a soft dough.

3 Turn onto a floured board (use self-raising flour). Knead lightly. Roll out to form a rectangle about 1.5 cm thick.

4 Warm jam on the stove or in the microwave. Spread over dough. Roll up like a Swiss roll. Cut into 2 cm slices.

5 Place in a greased 18 cm sandwich tin, cut side up. Glaze with a little milk and bake for 15–20 minutes. Cool on wire rack. Serve warm with butter.

Sultana Scones

Preparation time: 25 minutes
Cooking time: 12 minutes
Makes 12

2 cups self-raising flour
30 g butter, cut into small pieces
⅓ cup caster sugar
¼ cup sultanas
1 egg, lightly beaten
150 mL milk

1 Preheat oven to very hot (220°C). Sift flour into a large bowl. Add butter and rub in lightly with fingertips.

2 Mix in sugar and sultanas. Combine egg and milk. Make a well in the centre of the flour. Pour in liquid all at once, reserving about a teaspoon for glazing. Mix quickly to a soft dough.

3 Turn onto a floured board (use self-raising flour). Knead lightly. Press or roll out to form a round about 2 cm thick.

4 Cut using a floured plain round cutter or cut into triangles using a floured knife. Place on a greased oven tray and glaze with milk. Bake for 10–12 minutes. Cool on wire rack. Serve buttered.

Cheese Herb Scroll

Preparation time: 35 minutes
Cooking time: 30 minutes
Makes 1 x 20 cm scroll

3 cups self-raising flour
pinch baking powder
45 g butter
²⁄₃ cup milk
¹⁄₃ cup water

Filling
1 cup shredded Cheddar cheese
¹⁄₂ cup grated Parmesan cheese
¹⁄₂ cup chopped parsley
1 tablespoon chopped fresh tarragon
1 tablespoon chopped oregano
1 tablespoon chopped rosemary leaves
15 g butter, softened
1 egg yolk, beaten
2 teaspoons water

1 Preheat oven to hot (200°C). In a large bowl, sift together the flour and baking powder; rub in the butter. Combine milk and water; thoroughly stir into dry ingredients to make a soft dough.
2 On lightly floured surface, gently knead dough until smooth.

Roll out to a 38 x 28 cm rectangle.
3 To make filling, combine the cheeses and herbs in a bowl. Spread soft butter thinly over rectangle to the edges; evenly sprinkle with the cheese mixture.
4 Roll up from one short end; cut crosswise into 10 equal slices. Arrange, cut side down, in greased and paper-lined 20 cm round cake tin.
5 Combine egg yolk and water; brush over slices. Bake 25–30 minutes or until the Scroll is firm and browned. Serve warm.

Cheese Herb Scroll

25

Cheese and Bacon Scone Round

Preparation time: 35 minutes
Cooking time: 15 minutes
Makes 8 wedges

2 cups self-raising flour, sifted
30 g butter, cut into small pieces
1/2 cup shredded Cheddar cheese
2 rashers rindless bacon, finely chopped
1/2 cup milk
1/2 cup water

1/2 cup shredded Cheddar cheese, extra
cayenne pepper

1 Preheat oven to very hot (220°C). Place flour in a bowl. Add butter and rub in with fingertips.

2 Stir in cheese and bacon. Combine milk and water. Make a well in centre of mixture. Pour in liquid all at once, reserving 1 teaspoon.

3 Mix to a soft dough. Turn onto a floured surface (use self-raising flour). Knead lightly. Press or roll out to form a 20 cm round.

4 Place round on greased baking tray. Using a floured knife cut two thirds of the way through to make 8 wedges. Glaze with remaining liquid. Sprinkle with extra cheese and a little cayenne.

5 Bake for 10–12 minutes or until scones sound hollow when tapped.

Cheese and Bacon Scone Round

Cheese Horseshoe

Preparation time: 40
   minutes
Cooking time: 20
   minutes
Serves 8

2 cups self-raising flour
30 g butter, cut into
   small pieces
½ cup milk
½ cup water

Filling
1 cup shredded Cheddar
   cheese
4 gherkins, chopped
½ small onion, chopped
¼ cup chopped
   capsicum
8 stuffed olives, chopped
½ cup shredded
   Cheddar cheese, extra

1   Preheat oven to very
hot (220°C). Sift flour
into a large bowl. Add
butter and rub in lightly
with fingertips.
2   Combine milk and
water. Make a well in
the centre of the flour
and pour in liquid all at
once. Mix quickly to a
soft dough.
3   Turn onto a floured
board (use self-raising
flour). Knead lightly.
Roll out to form a
rectangle about 1.5 cm
thick.
4   To prepare the filling,
combine all ingredients
except extra Cheddar
cheese.
5   Spread filling over
dough. Roll up like a
Swiss roll. Place seam
side down on a greased
oven tray.
6   Form into a
horseshoe shape. Slit
dough at 2 cm intervals
with a sharp knife.
Sprinkle with extra
cheese. Bake 15–20
minutes and serve hot.

HINT
Always have your
oven preheated to the
correct temperature,
which for scones is
usually very hot
(220°C). This will
allow for quick
cooking and a lighter
texture.

HINT
Wholemeal self-
raising flour can be
substituted for white
flour with good
results. However,
don't expect a very
light product.
Wholemeal scones
are always heavier in
texture. If you want
to try wholemeal
flour try using only
half the amount of
wholemeal and half
of the white.

Cheese Horseshoe

– TEACAKES –

Back: Traditional Tea Bun; front: Pecan Cinnamon Teacake

*T*eacakes are always firm family favourites. Serve them warm with butter or cooled and glazed for morning or afternoon tea. We have included fruit and spice teacakes, a traditional iced tea bun and fruit and nut glazed teacakes. All are quick and easy with good keeping qualities.

Traditional Tea Bun

Preparation time: 35 minutes
Cooking time: 20 minutes
Makes 1 bun

2¼ cups self-raising flour
¼ teaspoon ground cinnamon
60 g butter, cubed
2 tablespoons sultanas
1 tablespoon caster sugar
1 egg, beaten
½ cup milk

Icing
1 cup icing sugar
15 g butter
1 tablespoon hot water
¼ teaspoon imitation vanilla essence
pink food colouring, optional
glacé cherries and mixed peel, to decorate

1 Preheat oven to hot (200°C). Sift flour and cinnamon into a bowl. Add butter and rub in with fingertips.
2 Stir in sultanas and sugar. Combine egg and milk. Make a well in the centre of the flour mixture. Pour in liquid all at once and mix to a soft dough.
3 Knead lightly on a floured surface. Form into a half circle and, using scissors, make snips at 2 cm intervals around the curved edge.
4 Bake for 20 minutes or until bun sounds hollow when tapped. Cool on a wire rack.
5 To prepare icing, combine icing sugar, butter, water, vanilla and colouring (if using) in a bowl. Beat until smooth. Drizzle over bun and decorate with peel and cherries. Serve sliced with butter.

> ### HINT
> The dough may be split into three pieces. Roll each piece into a rope. Press ends together. Form into a plait. Press ends.

Pecan Cinnamon Teacake

Preparation time: 35 minutes
Cooking time: 30 minutes
Makes 1 x 20 cm cake

1 egg, separated
½ cup caster sugar
½ cup milk
1 teaspoon imitation vanilla essence
1 cup self-raising flour, sifted
¼ cup chopped pecans
30 g butter, melted

Topping
15 g butter, melted
1 tablespoon caster sugar
¼ teaspoon cinnamon
¼ teaspoon nutmeg

1 Preheat oven to moderate (180°C). Beat egg white until stiff peaks form. Add egg yolk. Gradually add sugar, beating well after each addition.
2 Combine milk and vanilla. Add to egg mixture a little at a time.
3 Fold in flour, pecans and butter. Pour into a greased and floured 20 cm sandwich tin.
4 Bake 25–30 minutes. Transfer cake to a wire rack to cool completely.
5 To prepare topping, brush hot cake with butter. Combine all remaining ingredients and sprinkle evenly over top of cake. Serve warm or cold with butter.

Walnut and Pear Teacake

Preparation time: 40 minutes
Cooking time: 1 hour
Makes 1 loaf

2 large pears, peeled, cored and finely chopped
2 eggs, beaten
1/3 cup milk
2/3 cup bran cereal (not flakes)
1 teaspoon imitation vanilla essence
1 cup plain flour
1/2 cup wholemeal plain flour
1/2 cup firmly packed brown sugar
1 teaspoon baking powder
1/2 teaspoon bicarbonate of soda
1/4 teaspoon ground nutmeg
60 g butter
2/3 cup chopped walnuts

1 Preheat oven to moderate (180°C). In a large bowl combine pears, eggs, milk, bran cereal and vanilla. Mix well, cover and let stand 10 minutes.
2 Combine flours, sugar, baking powder, bicarbonate of soda and nutmeg.
3 Rub butter into flour mixture until crumbly. Add cereal mixture and nuts and stir until just moistened.

4 Spoon into a greased, lightly floured 14 x 21 cm loaf tin. Bake until skewer inserted in centre comes out clean, about 1 hour.
5 Cool 5 minutes in tin; turn out onto rack and cool completely. Serve buttered.

Fruity Glazed Teacake

Preparation time: 40 minutes
Cooking time: 45 minutes
Makes 1 x 20 cm cake

3/4 cup mixed dried fruit
3/4 cup sugar
1 tablespoon butter
3/4 cup boiling water
1 egg
1 3/4 cups self-raising flour
1 teaspoon cinnamon

Glaze
3/4 cup icing sugar, sifted
1 tablespoon fruit juice
1 tablespoon chopped nuts

1 Preheat oven to moderate (180°C). In large bowl, combine fruit, sugar and butter. Pour in boiling water and mix well. Cool slightly and then beat in egg.

2 Sift together flour and cinnamon; gradually beat into fruit mixture until well combined. Spread the mixture into a greased and floured

Back: Fruity Glazed Teacake; front: Walnut and Pear Teacake

20 cm baba tin.
3 Bake until golden brown and skewer inserted in centre comes out clean, 40–45 minutes. Briefly cool in tin; turn out and cool completely on rack.
4 To make glaze, stir together icing sugar and fruit juice until smooth. Spread over cake, allowing some to drip down the sides. Sprinkle with nuts. Serve teacake sliced and buttered.

Back: Fruit and Nut Teacake; front: Tutti Frutti Teacake

Fruit and Nut Teacake

Preparation time: 40 minutes
Cooking time: 50 minutes
Makes 1 x 23 cm cake

Topping
1 *cup plain flour, sifted*
$^1/_2$ *teaspoon cinnamon*
$^1/_4$ *teaspoon grated nutmeg*
90 *g butter at room temperature*
$^1/_3$ *cup brown sugar*
$^1/_4$ *cup finely chopped pecans*

Cake
$^1/_2$ *cup finely chopped pecans*
$^3/_4$ *cup chopped sultanas*
rind of 1 orange
2 *cups plain flour, sifted*
1 *cup sugar*
1 *teaspoon bicarbonate of soda*
125 *g butter at room temperature*
1 *cup milk*
2 *eggs*

1 To prepare topping, combine flour, cinnamon and nutmeg in a bowl. Add butter and rub in using fingertips until mixture resembles breadcrumbs. Stir in sugar and nuts. Set aside.
2 To prepare cake, preheat oven to moderate (180°C). Combine nuts, sultanas and orange rind in a small bowl. Set aside.
3 Mix flour, sugar and soda together in a large bowl. Add butter and milk and beat with an electric beater for 2 minutes.
4 Add eggs and continue beating for a further 2 minutes. Blend in nut and fruit mixture.
5 Pour into a greased and paper-lined 23 cm square cake tin. Smooth top. Sprinkle evenly with topping mixture.
6 Bake for 45–50 minutes or until cake is cooked when tested with a skewer. Turn out onto a cake cooler.

HINT
When a recipe calls for a lined cake tin, use greaseproof paper. Always grease this paper and dust with flour to ensure the cake will not stick.

Tutti Frutti Teacake

Preparation time: 40 minutes
Cooking time: 50 minutes
Makes 1 loaf

1 *cup wholemeal plain flour*
$^1/_2$ *cup self-raising white flour*
$^1/_2$ *teaspoon baking powder*
60 *g butter*
$^1/_3$ *cup brown sugar*
$^1/_2$ *cup chopped dried apricots*
$^1/_4$ *cup chopped walnuts*
$^1/_2$ *cup quartered glacé cherries*
1 *egg, beaten*
$^1/_3$ *cup plain yoghurt*
2 *tablespoons milk*
1 *tablespoon warmed honey to glaze*

1 Preheat oven to moderate (180°C). Sift flours and baking powder into a large bowl. Add butter and rub in lightly with fingertips.
2 Stir in sugar, apricots, walnuts and cherries. Combine egg, yoghurt and milk and mix well. Pour egg mixture into flour mixture and mix quickly to a soft batter.
3 Spread mixture into a greased and lined 14 x 21 cm loaf tin. Bake for about 45–50 minutes until a skewer inserted in the centre comes out clean.
4 Cool 5 minutes in tin; turn out onto rack and peel off paper. Brush warmed honey over top to glaze; then cool completely. Wrap and store overnight before serving.

Apple and Cinnamon Teacake

Preparation time: 35 minutes
Cooking time: 1 hour
Makes 1 x 20 cm cake

180 g butter
½ cup brown sugar

grated rind of 1 lemon
3 eggs
1 cup self-raising flour
½ cup wholemeal plain flour
1 teaspoon ground cinnamon
½ cup milk
½ cup sultanas
1 apple, peeled, cored and sliced

1 tablespoon apricot jam, warmed
cinnamon sugar (see Note)

1 Preheat oven to moderate (180°C). Cream butter and sugar together until creamy. Beat in rind. Add eggs one at a time, beating

Apple and Cinnamon Teacake

well after each.
2 Sift flours and cinnamon together. Fold into creamed mixture alternately with milk. Stir in sultanas.
3 Pour mixture into a greased 20 cm springform pan. Arrange the apple slices, rounded side up, in a spoke pattern in the batter.
4 Bake for 55–60 minutes. Brush with jam and sprinkle with cinnamon sugar. Remove from tin and cool on a wire rack.
Note. Cinnamon sugar is available from supermarkets.

Alternatively, mix together 1 tablespoon caster sugar with $\frac{1}{2}$ teaspoon ground cinnamon.

– *SWEET & SAVOURY LOAVES* –

*Clockwise from back: Apple Orange Loaf,
Citrus Nut Loaf and Date and Walnut Loaf*

Quick loaves like these are wholesome and versatile. Our sweet loaves are fruity and perfect for morning or afternoon tea, served with lashings of butter. The savoury loaves are ideal served with soups, casseroles and salads.

All these treats keep for several days in an airtight container. You will find they freeze and reheat well too.

Apple Orange Loaf

Preparation time: 50 minutes
Cooking time: 50 minutes
Makes 1 loaf

90 g butter
2/3 cup sugar
2 eggs
1 cup plain flour
1 cup wholemeal plain flour
1 teaspoon baking powder
1/2 teaspoon bicarbonate of soda
1 cup finely chopped apples
1/2 cup currants
1/4 cup chopped walnuts
2 teaspoons grated orange rind
1/4 cup milk

1 Preheat oven to moderate (180°C). Cream butter and sugar together until light and fluffy. Add eggs one at a time, beating well after each addition.
2 Stir in sifted flours, baking powder, bicarbonate of soda, apples, currants, walnuts and rind alternately with milk.
3 Spread into a greased 15 x 25 cm loaf tin and bake for about 50 minutes or until loaf is cooked when tested.
4 Allow to cool in tin for 5 minutes. Then turn onto a wire rack to cool completely.

Citrus Nut Loaf

Preparation time: 50 minutes
Cooking time: 50 minutes
Makes 1 loaf

90 g butter
2/3 cup sugar
2 eggs
1 1/2 cups plain flour
1 teaspoon baking powder
1/2 teaspoon bicarbonate of soda
1/4 cup orange juice
1/4 cup lemon juice
1/2 cup chopped pecans

1 Preheat oven to moderate (180°C). Cream butter and sugar together until light and fluffy. Add eggs one at a time, beating well after each addition.
2 Stir in sifted flour, baking powder and bicarbonate of soda alternately with combined fruit juices. Stir in nuts.
3 Spread into a greased 15 x 25 cm loaf tin. Bake for 50 minutes or until loaf is cooked when tested.
4 Allow to cool in tin for 5 minutes. Turn on to a wire rack to cool.

Date and Walnut Loaf

Preparation time: 40 minutes
Cooking time: 40 minutes
Makes 2 loaves

125 g butter
1 cup brown sugar
2 eggs
300 mL milk
1 1/2 cups chopped dates
1 cup chopped walnuts
3 cups self-raising flour, sifted

1 Preheat oven to moderate (180°C). Cream butter and sugar in a bowl. Add eggs one at a time, beating well after each addition.
2 Blend in milk, dates and walnuts. Fold flour in lightly. Pour into two greased 14 x 21 cm loaf tins.
3 Bake for 35–40 minutes. Remove from tins and cool on a cake cooler. Serve sliced, warm or cold, with butter. Store in an airtight container.

Herbed Carrot Cornmeal Loaf

Preparation time: 35 minutes
Cooking time: 1 hour
Makes 1 loaf

1 cup cornmeal (polenta)
1 cup self-raising flour
1 tablespoon sugar
1 cup shredded carrot
1 tablespoon chopped parsley
2 teaspoons chopped chives
2 teaspoons dried marjoram leaves
1 cup sour cream
2 eggs
125 g butter, melted

1 Preheat oven to moderate (180°C). In a large bowl combine cornmeal, flour and sugar. In a separate bowl, mix together carrot and remaining ingredients.
2 Make a well in centre of dry ingredients; add carrot mixture and quickly stir until just moistened (do not overmix).
3 Spoon into a lightly greased and floured 14 x 21 cm loaf tin. Bake in a moderate oven until skewer inserted comes out clean, about 1 hour.
4 Cool 5 minutes in tin; turn out onto rack. Serve warm or cooled with soups and casseroles.

Tomato Basil Bread

Preparation time: 50 minutes
Cooking time: 1 hour
Makes 1 loaf

125 g butter
1 tablespoon tomato paste
1 tablespoon brown sugar
2 eggs
2 cups plain flour
1 teaspoon baking powder
1 teaspoon bicarbonate of soda
1 teaspoon dried basil
½ cup tomato juice
60 g Cheddar cheese, shredded

1 Preheat oven to moderate (180°C). Cream butter, tomato paste, sugar and eggs until light and fluffy.
2 Sift together flour, baking powder and bicarbonate of soda; stir in basil.
3 Gradually stir dry ingredients into creamed mixture alternately with tomato juice. Fold in cheese.
4 Spoon into greased lightly floured 15 x 21 cm loaf tin. Bake until bread springs back when touched and skewer inserted in centre comes out clean, about 1 hour.
5 Cool 5 minutes in tin; turn out onto rack and

cool completely. Wrap and store overnight.

Garlic Cheese Casserole Bread

Preparation time: 35 minutes
Cooking time: 1 hour
Makes 1 round

Left: Tomato Basil Bread; right: Herbed Carrot Cornmeal Loaf and front: Garlic Cheese Casserole Bread

185 g butter
3 eggs
2 cloves garlic, crushed
1½ cups self-raising flour
¾ cup plain flour
½ teaspoon bicarbonate of soda
1 cup sour cream
125 g Edam or Gouda cheese, shredded

1 Preheat oven to moderate (180°C). In large bowl, cream the butter until smooth; beat in eggs and garlic. Sift together flours and bicarbonate of soda; gradually stir into egg mixture alternately with sour cream until well combined. Stir in the shredded cheese.

2 Spoon into a greased lightly floured 20 cm cake tin. Bake for 50-60 minutes.

3 Cool 5 minutes before turning out onto rack. Serve warm with lashings of butter.

41

Banana Bar.

Banana Bar

Preparation time: 30 minutes
Cooking time: 45 minutes
Makes 1 bar

60 g butter
2/3 cup caster sugar
1 teaspoon vanilla essence
2 bananas, well mashed
1 egg, lightly beaten
1 1/2 cups self-raising flour
1/2 cup milk

1 Preheat oven to moderate 180°C. Brush 9 x 23 cm loaf tin with melted butter or oil. Coat base and sides with flour; shake excess.
2 Using electric beaters, beat butter and sugar in a small mixing bowl until light and creamy. Add mashed banana; beat until combined. Add egg gradually, beating thoroughly after each addition. Add essence; beat until combined.
3 Transfer mixture to large mixing bowl. Using a metal spoon, fold in sifted flour alternately with milk. Stir until just combined and mixture is smooth.
4 Pour mixture into prepared tin; smooth surface. Bake for 45 minutes or until a skewer comes out clean when inserted into the centre of cake. Leave cake in tin 5 minutes, then turn onto a wire rack to cool. Serve buttered, or top with lemon icing.

Carrot and Zucchini Loaf

*Preparation time: 50
minutes*
*Cooking time: 45
minutes*
Makes 1 loaf

90 g butter
¾ cup brown sugar
2 teaspoons grated
orange rind
2 eggs
1½ cups self-raising
flour
½ teaspoon ground
cinnamon

2 tablespoons orange
juice
2 tablespoons milk
½ cup chopped walnuts
½ cup shredded carrot
½ cup shredded zucchini

Frosting
60 g spreadable cream
cheese
3 tablespoons icing
sugar
1 tablespoon orange
juice
2 teaspoons grated
orange rind

1 Preheat oven to
moderate (180°C).
Cream butter and sugar together until light and
fluffy. Beat in rind. Add
eggs one at a time,
beating well after each
addition. Stir in all
remaining ingredients.
2 Pour into a greased
15 x 25 cm loaf tin.
Bake for 45 minutes or
until loaf is cooked
when tested.
3 Allow to cool in tin
for 5 minutes. Turn
onto a wire rack to cool
completely.
4 To make frosting,
beat cream cheese, icing
sugar, orange juice and
rind until smooth.
Spread over cold cake.

Carrot and Zucchini Loaf

Prune and Nut Loaf

Preparation time: 40 minutes
Cooking time: 1 hour
Makes 1 loaf

1 cup wholemeal plain
  flour, sifted
1 cup plain flour, sifted
1 cup rolled oats
½ cup caster sugar
1 teaspoon mixed spice
1 teaspoon bicarbonate
  of soda
125 g butter, cubed
2 eggs
½ cup sour cream
¼ cup milk
1 cup chopped pitted
  prunes
⅓ cup walnut halves

1 Preheat oven to moderate (180°C). Place flours, oats, sugar, mixed spice and bicarbonate of soda in a large bowl and mix well. Rub in butter with fingertips until mixture resembles breadcrumbs.
2 Whisk eggs and sour cream together in a small bowl. Make a well in the centre of the flour mixture. Pour in egg mixture and milk and mix to a stiff but moist dough. Stir in prunes and nuts.
3 Spoon mixture into a greased 14 x 21 cm loaf tin. Smooth top and decorate with extra walnut halves if desired.
4 Bake for about 1 hour or until cooked.
5 Cool loaf in tin for 5 minutes. Turn out onto wire rack to cool completely. Store in an airtight container.

HINT
For a change of shape, bake batter in a 20 cm square tin for 25–30 minutes. Cut into squares to serve.

HINT
Always allow cake to rest in the tin after cooking for 1–2 minutes before turning out onto a wire rack to cool. This ensures that cake will not stick to base of tin or fall apart as you turn it out.

Prune and Nut Loaf

— TEATIME FAVOURITES —

Left to right: Butter Cake, Pineapple Upside-down Cake and Rock Cakes

There are many different types of cakes but the ones included here all have one thing in common — everybody loves them. Plain or fancy, iced or buttered, they make morning or afternoon tea a special event.

To achieve success each time with baking start with the best ingredients. Always weigh or measure ingredients accurately — use standard measuring cups and spoons. Follow the steps of the recipe carefully, preheat your oven and choose the correct size tin.

Baking times will vary slightly according to your oven and the type of baking ware used. When a cake is ready, it should have an even colour, be firm when touched in the centre and should shrink away from the sides of the tin. After baking, cool your cake in the tin for about 5 minutes before turning out onto a wire rack to cool completely.

These cakes freeze well. They are best frozen unfilled and without icing. Place cake on a tray without covering. When frozen, wrap in plastic film and good quality foil, excluding as much air as possible. Store in an additional rigid container for added protection. Cakes freeze well for up to 3 months.

To thaw, loosen wrapping and stand at room temperature for 1–3 hours depending on size.

Butter Cake

Preparation time: 40 minutes
Cooking time: 45 minutes
Makes 1 cake

125 g butter
½ cup caster sugar
½ teaspoon imitation vanilla essence
2 eggs
2 cups self-raising flour, sifted
½ cup milk

Vanilla Icing
1 cup icing sugar
15 g butter
½ teaspoon imitation vanilla essence
1–2 tablespoons hot water

1 Preheat oven to moderate (180°C). Cream butter and sugar together until light and fluffy. Beat in vanilla. Add eggs one at a time, beating well after each addition.
2 Fold flour gently into creamed mixture alternately with milk, beginning and ending with flour.
3 Spoon mixture into a greased 10 x 20 cm loaf tin. Bake for 40–45 minutes. Turn out onto a wire rack and allow to cool.
4 To prepare Vanilla Icing, beat all ingredients together until smooth. Spread over cooled cake.

HINT

It is best if butter for cake making is at room temperature. If possible leave measured butter out of the refrigerator overnight.

Rock Cakes

Preparation time: 30 minutes
Cooking time: 15 minutes
Makes about 20

2 cups self-raising flour, sifted
90 g butter or margarine, cut into pieces
½ cup caster sugar
½ cup mixed fruit
1 tablespoon chopped mixed nuts, optional
½ teaspoon ground ginger
1 egg
¼ cup milk

1 Preheat oven to hot (200°C). Place flour in a large bowl. Add butter and rub in with fingertips until mixture resembles breadcrumbs.
2 Mix in sugar, fruit, nuts and ginger. Whisk eggs into milk and add to dry ingredients. Mix to a stiff dough.
3 Place mixture in small, rough heaps on greased oven trays. Bake for 10–15 minutes or until golden brown. Transfer to a cake cooler to cool. Serve buttered.

Pineapple Upside-down Cake

Preparation time: 45 minutes
Cooking time: 40 minutes
Makes 1 cake

Base
60 g butter, at room temperature
1/2 cup brown sugar
4 slices canned pineapple, drained and halved
12 glacé cherries

Cake
125 g butter
1/2 cup caster sugar
2 eggs
1 teaspoon imitation vanilla essence
11/2 cups self-raising flour, sifted
1/2 cup milk

1 To prepare base, cream butter and sugar together in a small bowl. Spread over the base of a 20 cm ring tin lined with greased greaseproof paper. Arrange pineapple and cherries decoratively over base. Set aside.
2 To prepare cake, preheat oven to moderate (180°C). Cream butter and sugar together until light and fluffy. Add eggs one at a time, beating well after each addition. Stir in the vanilla essence.
3 Fold flour into creamed mixture alternately with milk, beginning and ending with flour.
4 Spread cake mixture carefully over base. Bake about 40 minutes. Allow to cool in tin for 15 minutes before turning out onto a wire rack to cool completely.

Chocolate Sponge

Preparation time: 30 minutes
Cooking time: 15 minutes
Makes 1 cake

3 eggs, separated
3/4 cup caster sugar
1 cup self-raising flour, sifted

60 g chocolate, melted
3 tablespoons water

Filling
300 mL cream
1/2 teaspoon cocoa
30 g chocolate, melted

1 Preheat oven to moderate (180°C). Place egg whites in a clean, dry bowl. Beat until stiff peaks form. Gradually add sugar and beat until thick and glossy.
2 Add egg yolks and beat well. Gently fold in flour, followed by chocolate and water. Divide mixture evenly between two greased and floured 20 cm sandwich tins.
3 Bake for 12–15 minutes or until cake springs back when touched. Remove from tins. Cool on a wire rack.
4 To prepare filling, whip cream and cocoa together. When beginning to thicken, pour in chocolate. Continue whipping until cream is a spreadable consistency.
5 Spread the filling over the top of one cake. Place the other cake on top and decorate with icing sugar and strawberries if liked.

Note. If cream is cold and chocolate is warm, chocolate chips will form in the cream during whipping.

Chocolate Sponge and Cream Horns

Cream Horns

Preparation time: 35
  minutes
Cooking time: 20
  minutes
Makes 8

1 *sheet frozen, ready-
  rolled puff pastry,
  thawed*
½ *cup cream*
½ *teaspoon brandy*
½ *teaspoon grated
  orange rind*
1 *orange, segmented*
icing sugar

1 Preheat oven to hot
(220°C). Brush one side
of pastry with a little
water. Cut pastry sheet
into 5 mm strips.
2 Lightly grease cream
horn moulds (see Note).
Starting at the pointed
end of the mould, wind
pastry around until
almost covered (you will
need about 2 strips).
Overlay edges of strips
slightly.
3 Lay moulds flat on a
baking tray. Bake for
15–20 minutes or until
golden and crisp.
4 Remove horns from
moulds. Cool on a wire
rack.
5 Whip cream with
brandy and rind. Spoon
or pipe into cool horns.
Garnish with an orange
segment. Serve dusted
with icing sugar.
Note. Buy cream horn
moulds from speciality
kitchen shops.

49

1 Gradually add sugar to beaten egg whites and beat until thick and glossy.

2 Using a large metal spoon, gently fold in flour.

3 Carefully divide mixture evenly between two sandwich tins.

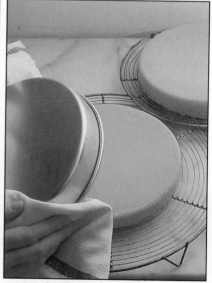

4 Stand for a few minutes after baking; then turn out onto a cake cooler.

Never-Fail Sponge

Preparation time: 30
  minutes
Cooking time: 15
  minutes
Makes 1 cake

3 eggs, separated
¾ cup caster sugar
1 cup self-raising flour,
  sifted
3 tablespoons water
½ cup strawberry or
  other jam
300 mL cream, whipped

2 *tablespoons icing*
  sugar

1 Preheat oven to
moderate (180°C). Place
egg whites in a clean,
dry bowl. Beat until stiff
peaks form. Gradually
add sugar and beat until
thick and glossy.
2 Add egg yolks and
beat well. Gently fold in
flour; then stir in water.
3 Divide mixture evenly
between 2 greased and
floured 20 cm sandwich
tins. Bake for 10–15
minutes or until cake

springs back when
touched.
4 Remove from tins.
Cool on a cake cooler.
When cool, spread with
jam followed by cream.
Sandwich layers
together and decorate
top of cake with sifted
icing sugar.

HINT
Sponge cakes do not
keep well, so make
them the day you
intend to serve them.

Never-Fail Sponge

Caramel Cake

Preparation time: 55 minutes
Cooking time: 35 minutes
Makes 1 cake

Syrup
1 *cup sugar*
³/₄ *cup boiling water*

Cake
180 g *butter or margarine*
¹/₂ *cup brown sugar*
3 *eggs, separated*
1 *teaspoon imitation vanilla essence*
¹/₂ *cup Syrup*
3 *cups self-raising flour, sifted*
³/₄ *cup milk*

Frosting
60 g *butter, at room temperature*
2 *cups icing sugar*
2–3 *tablespoons Syrup*
1 *teaspoon imitation vanilla essence*

1 To prepare Syrup, heat sugar in a saucepan over a very low heat. Stir until melted and a rich caramel colour. Remove from heat. Gradually stir in boiling water, being careful to avoid splashes. Cool.
2 To prepare Cake, preheat oven to moderate (180°C). Cream butter and sugar together until light and fluffy. Add egg yolks and vanilla and beat well. Blend in ¹/₂ cup cooled Syrup.
3 Fold flour into creamed mixture alternately with milk. Beat egg whites until stiff. Fold gently into batter.
4 Divide mixture between two greased 20 cm sandwich tins. Bake for 35 minutes. Turn onto wire racks to cool.
5 To prepare Frosting, cream butter and icing sugar together until smooth and creamy. Gradually add Syrup and vanilla and beat well.
6 Join cakes together with half of the frosting. Spread remaining frosting on top. Decorate with walnuts or hazelnuts.

HINT
Test cakes to see if they are cooked by inserting a skewer in the centre of the cake. If the skewer comes out clean and dry, the cake is cooked. Other ways to tell if a cake is cooked are when the cake comes away from the sides of the tin and when the cake springs back when pressed gently with the finger.

Ginger Cake

Preparation time: 40 minutes
Cooking time: 40 minutes
Makes 1 cake

45 g *butter*
¹/₂ *cup caster sugar*
2 *eggs*
1 *tablespoon golden syrup*

1 cup self-raising flour
1½ teaspoons ground
  ginger
½ cup milk
½ teaspoon bicarbonate
  of soda
½ cup cream, whipped
icing sugar

1 Preheat oven to moderate (180°C). Cream butter and sugar together until light and fluffy. Add eggs one at a time, beating well after each addition. Blend in the golden syrup.

2 Sift flour and ginger together. Fold into creamed mixture alternately with combined milk and soda.

3 Pour milk into a greased 20 cm round cake tin. Bake for 40 minutes; turn onto a wire rack and cool.

4 Split cake. Spread one half with cream. Top with remaining cake layer and dust top with icing sugar.

HINT
Curdling of the cake batter will generally not spoil the finished result.

Left: Caramel Cake; right: Ginger Cake

Swiss Roll

Preparation time: 30
  minutes
Cooking time: 10
  minutes
Makes 1 Swiss roll
  (about 10 slices)

3 eggs, separated
½ cup caster sugar
¾ cup self-raising flour,
  sifted
2 tablespoons hot milk
caster sugar, extra
2 tablespoons
  strawberry jam
300 mL cream, whipped

1 Preheat oven to very
hot (220°C). Place egg
whites in a clean, dry
bowl. Beat until stiff
peaks form. Gradually
add sugar and beat until
thick and glossy.
2 Add egg yolks one at
a time, beating well
after each addition.
Lightly fold in flour
with milk until
combined.
3 Pour into a greased
and lined Swiss roll tin.
Bake for 8–10 minutes.
4 Turn out onto
greaseproof paper which
has been sprinkled with
extra caster sugar. Trim
all edges. Roll up
immediately, taking
paper with cake. Allow
to cool on a wire rack.
5 When cool unroll
cake. Spread with jam,
followed by cream. Re-
roll without paper.

Serve sliced with extra
cream.

Chocolate Swiss Roll

Replace 2 tablespoons
of flour in the recipe for
Swiss Roll with 2
tablespoons of cocoa.
Continue as directed.
Delete jam from filling.

HINT
When rolling Swiss
Roll it helps if cake is
placed on a clean tea-
towel for easy
rolling.

HINT
Butter is better than
margarine for making
cakes as it gives the
best flavour and
improves the keeping
qualities of the cake.
However, margarine
can be substituted.

Left to right:

Almond and Hazelnut Torte (page 58), Classic Swiss Roll, Chocolate Swiss Roll

Lamingtons

Lamingtons

Preparation time: 1
   hour, plus overnight
Cooking time: 30
   minutes
Makes 24

125 g butter
¾ cup caster sugar
2 eggs
½ teaspoon imitation
   vanilla essence
2 cups self-raising flour,
   sifted
½ cup milk
2½ cups desiccated
   coconut

Mock Cream
2 tablespoons water
¼ cup sugar
60 g butter
few drops imitation
   vanilla essence

Chocolate Icing
3 cups icing sugar
¼ cup cocoa
⅓ cup boiling water
1 teaspoon butter
few drops imitation
   vanilla essence

1 Preheat oven to
moderate (180°C).
Cream butter and sugar
together until light and
fluffy. Add eggs one at a
time, beating well after
each addition. Add
vanilla essence.
2 Fold in flour
alternately with milk.
When mixed pour into a
greased and lined 20 x
30 x 4 cm oven tray.
3 Bake for 30 minutes

or until cooked when
tested. Cool on a wire
rack. Store overnight.
4 To prepare Mock
Cream, place water and
sugar in a small
saucepan. Cook,
stirring, until mixture
boils. Remove from
heat. Cool.
5 Cream butter and
vanilla in a small bowl
using an electric beater.
Pour syrup in a thin
stream into butter. Beat
well.
6 To prepare Chocolate
Icing, sift icing sugar
and cocoa into a bowl.
Stir in remaining
ingredients. Beat until
smooth.
7 Use immediately.
Keep at the correct
consistency by standing
over a bowl of hot
water.
8 To assemble, split
cake horizontally.
Spread base with Mock
Cream. Place other layer
on top.
9 Cut into 24 pieces.
Dip into Chocolate
Icing. Roll immediately
in coconut. Stand on a
wire rack until set. Store
in an airtight container.

Rainbow Cake

Preparation time: 1
   hour
Cooking time: 30
   minutes
Makes 1 cake

4 eggs
1 cup caster sugar
30 g butter
1 cup hot milk
1 teaspoon imitation
   vanilla essence
2 cups self-raising flour,
   sifted
red food colouring
1 tablespoon cocoa
2 tablespoons warm
   milk, extra
300 mL cream

Icing
1½ cups icing sugar
6–7 tablespoons water
½ teaspoon imitation
   vanilla essence
few drops red food
   colouring

1 Preheat oven to
moderate (180°C). Beat
eggs, gradually adding
sugar, until thick and
pale. Melt butter in hot
milk. Stir in vanilla.
2 Fold flour into egg
mixture alternately with
milk. Divide mixture
into 3 portions.
3 Colour 1 portion
with red food colouring
until pink. Mix cocoa
with extra milk until
smooth. Add to next
portion and mix well.
Leave the remaining
portion plain.
4 Pour each portion
into a greased and lined
20 cm sandwich tin.
Bake for 25-30 minutes
or until cooked.
5 Turn cakes onto wire
racks and cool.
6 Whip cream and
spread half over plain

cake. Top with pink cake, spread remaining cream over. Top with the chocolate cake.

7 To prepare Icing, sift icing sugar into a bowl. Gradually add enough water to make a soft paste. Stir in vanilla. Set aside ¼ cup for decoration. Colour remainder to desired shade. (Or, icing can be left white if desired.) Set bowl over another filled with hot water to prevent setting.

8 Place cake on a cake cooler. Pour icing over so that it drips down and covers the sides. Quickly smooth top with a metal spatula or knife (see Note).

9 To decorate with a spider-web pattern, fit piping bag with a small plain nozzle. Fill with reserved plain icing. Starting at the centre, pipe a spiral out to the edge of cake. Working from the centre out to the edge, mark into 8 segments by dragging the point of a knife through icing. Divide the segments again by working from the edge into the centre.

Note. Dip spatula into hot water when smoothing icing.

Almond and Hazelnut Torte

Preparation time: 40 minutes
Cooking time: 40 minutes
Makes 1 x 23 cm cake

125 g butter
125 g chocolate, broken
1 cup sugar
4 eggs, separated
1 cup ground almonds
½ cup ground hazelnuts

1 Melt butter, chocolate and sugar together in a small saucepan. Cool.

2 Beat in egg yolks one at a time. Stir in nuts. Transfer mixture to a large bowl.

3 Beat egg whites until stiff peaks form. Fold gently into chocolate mixture.

4 Pour into a deep, greased and lined 23 cm round tin. Bake in a moderate oven (180°C) for 35–40 minutes, or until centre feels firm when pressed.

5 Allow to cool in tin for 5 minutes. Run a knife around the sides of the pan to loosen the cake. Turn onto a wire rack to cool completely. When cool, cut into wedges. Serve with whipped cream.

Rainbow Cake

Marble Cake

Preparation time: 50
   minutes
Cooking time: 45
   minutes
Makes 1 cake

125 g butter
½ cup caster sugar
2 eggs
½ teaspoon imitation
   vanilla essence
2 cups self-raising flour,
   sifted
½ cup milk
2 tablespoons cocoa
⅛ teaspoon bicarbonate
   of soda
1 tablespoon milk, extra
few drops red food
   colouring

Icing
1 cup icing sugar, sifted
15 g butter
1–2 tablespoons hot
   water
¼ teaspoon imitation
   vanilla essence
few drops red food
   colouring, extra

1 Preheat oven to
moderate (180°C).
Cream butter and sugar
together until light and
fluffy. Add eggs one at a
time, beating well after
each addition. Mix in
vanilla. Fold in flour
alternately with milk.
2 Divide mixture into 3
separate bowls. Add
cocoa, soda and milk to
one, blending well.
Leave one plain. Stir
food colouring into the
remaining bowl until the
desired colour is
achieved.
3 Drop alternate
colours into a greased
and floured 9 x 23 cm
loaf tin until all batter is
used.
4 Draw a skewer or
knife through the batter
in circles to streak the
colours. Bake for 40–45
minutes or until cooked
when tested with a
skewer.
5 Cool in tin for 5
minutes. Turn onto a
wire rack to cool
completely.
6 To prepare icing,
blend all ingredients
together until smooth.
Spread over the top of
cake. Store in an airtight
container.

HINT
When folding
ingredients into a
cake batter, do so
with a very light
hand to allow for
maximum rising of
the finished cake.

HINT
Always handle a hot
cooked sponge as
little as possible. Use
a knife to loosen cake
in tin and turn out
onto a tea-towel
placed over a cake
rack.

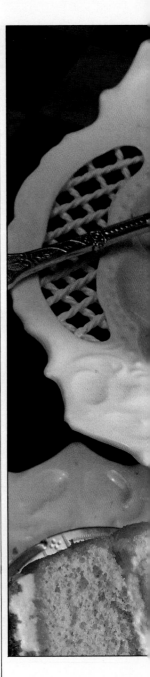

Marble Cake

Chocolate Carrot Cake

Preparation time: 30 minutes
Cooking time: 45 minutes
Makes 1 cake

1½ cups self-raising flour
¼ cup cocoa
1 teaspoon cinnamon
¼ teaspoon nutmeg
pinch mixed spice
½ cup chopped walnuts
½ cup raisins
⅓ cup shredded coconut
3 eggs
¾ cup brown sugar
½ cup oil
125 g milk chocolate, melted
3 cups shredded carrot

Icing
250 g cream cheese
125 g milk chocolate, melted
2 cups icing sugar, sifted
carrot slivers to decorate

1 Sift flour, cocoa, cinnamon, nutmeg and mixed spice into a large bowl. Mix in walnuts, raisins and coconut.
2 Whisk together eggs, brown sugar and oil until smooth. Beat in melted chocolate. Fold in carrots. Fold into flour mixture.
3 Pour into a greased and lined 23 x 32 cm slab tin. Bake in a moderately slow oven (160°C) for 45 minutes or until cooked. Cool for 15 minutes. Remove from tin.
4 To prepare Icing, beat cream cheese until smooth. Blend in chocolate and icing sugar. Chill until cake is cold. Spread over cake. Decorate with carrot slivers. Cut cake into squares to serve.

Chocolate Carrot Cake

INDEX